Hurricane!

BY ELIZABETH RAUM

AMICUS HIGH INTEREST • AMICUS INK

Amicus High Interest and Amicus Ink are published by Amicus
P.O. Box 1329, Mankato, MN 56002
www.amicuspublishing.us

Library of Congress Cataloging-in-Publication Data
Names: Raum, Elizabeth, author.
Title: Hurricane! / by Elizabeth Raum.
Description: Mankato, MN : Amicus, [2017] | Series: Natural
  disasters | Audience: K to Grade 3. | Includes index.
Identifiers: LCCN 2015031585 (print) | LCCN 2016002856
  (ebook) | ISBN 9781607539919 (library binding) | ISBN
  9781607539971 (ebook) | ISBN 9781681520841 (pbk.)
  | ISBN 9781607539971 (pdf)
Subjects: LCSH: Hurricanes—Juvenile literature.
Classification: LCC QC944.2 .R3785 2017 (print) | LCC
  QC944.2 (ebook) | DDC 551.55/2-dc23
LC record available at http://lccn.loc.gov/2015031585

Editor: Wendy Dieker
Series Designer: Kathleen Petelinsek
Book Designer: Tracy Myers
Photo Researcher: Rebecca Bernin

Photo Credits: Handout/Handout/Getty Images cover;
HaraldEWeiss/iStock 5; Stefano Politi Markovina/Alamy
Stock Photo 6; NASA 9; ZUMA Press, Inc/Alamy Stock Photo
10; ChinaFotoPress/Getty Images 12-13; firoz ahmed/
Demotix/Corbis 14; Yuri Cortez/AFP/Getty Images 17;
michaelbwatkins/iStock 18; FashionStock.com/Shutterstock 21;
Mark Elias/Bloomberg/Getty Images 22; Molly Riley/Reuters/
Corbis 25; hillwoman2/iStock 26; Charles W Luzier/Reuters/
Corbis 29

Printed in the United States of America.

HC 10 9 8 7 6 5 4 3 2 1
PB 10 9 8 7 6 5 4 3 2 1

Table of Contents

The Biggest Storm

Rain pours down. The wind is blowing hard. You carry a box of photos to the car. You look back at the house. Plywood covers the windows. It's time to go. You join a line of cars going inland, away from the storm. Hurricanes are the world's biggest storms. And a big one is charging toward the coast. You'll be safest if you leave until it passes.

Hurricanes are storms with heavy rains and very high wind.

These clouds show how warm air rises up. This rising air can make strong hurricane winds.

How fast can hurricane winds blow?

Hurricanes form in warm ocean waters. The warm water rises into the air. It forms big, fluffy clouds. The clouds create wind. The warm waters act like fuel. They make the wind go faster and faster. The wind circles around the center. When winds reach 74 miles per hour (120 kph), the storm is a called a hurricane.

 They can reach 186 miles per hour (300 kph).

A Big, Bad Bagel

From up above in the sky, a hurricane looks like a bagel. The hole in the middle is the eye. The thick ring of clouds swirling around the eye is the **eye wall**. It has the strongest winds and the heaviest rain. When a hurricane hits land, it blows down trees and buildings. Hurricane rains cause floods. The winds blow rain and seawater onto the land.

 What happens when the eye hits land?

This image from space shows
a hurricane over the ocean.
The clouds swirl in a circle.

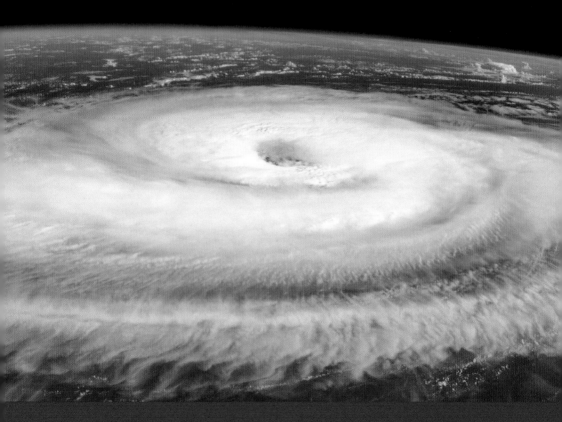

 It feels like the storm is over. It is not.
There are more winds coming.

These houses in Florida were destroyed by Hurricane Andrew in 1992.

 Do hurricanes kill people?

Some hurricanes are worse than others. A scale is used to measure them. It goes from **category** 1 to 5. At 1, large tree branches snap off. Houses lose roofs or siding. At category 5, most houses are destroyed. Power and water may be out for months. Category 5 storms are called super hurricanes.

 All hurricanes can be killers. People may drown in floods or be hit by flying **debris**.

Hurricane winds whip up huge waves. This is called a **storm surge**. The storm surge acts like a bulldozer along the shoreline. The water knocks down trees and power lines. It destroys houses, schools, and shops. It causes floods. People drown in the high waters. The storm surge causes terrible losses. It may take months or years to rebuild.

Huge waves of water can do much damage.

Homes were destroyed in Bangladesh during strong storms. It takes a long time to rebuild.

Q Is a cyclone the same as a hurricane?

Horrible Hurricanes

All hurricanes cause harm. Many of the worst ones have struck South Asia. There, hurricanes are called **cyclones**. In 1970, a cyclone hit Bangladesh. Storm surge waves reached 20 to 30 feet (6 to 9 m) high. Towns and cities flooded. Floods killed up to 500,000 people. It was the most deadly hurricane in history.

 Yes. Hurricanes are also called typhoons in other parts of the world.

In 1998, Hurricane Mitch struck Central America. It was a category 5 hurricane. About 50 inches (127 cm) of rain fell. The heavy rains caused floods and mudslides. Mitch left millions of people without homes. The storm wiped out crops. It ruined towns and cities. About 11,000 people died.

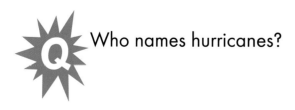 Who names hurricanes?

This man in Honduras studies damage done by Hurricane Mitch.

The World Meteorological Organization does. When a storm is really bad, like Mitch, the name is not used again.

In August 2005, Hurricane Katrina formed in the Atlantic Ocean. The storm moved into the Gulf of Mexico. It grew to a category 5 hurricane. As the storm hit land, it weakened to a category 3 storm. Trees and houses were knocked down. The storm surge flooded the city of New Orleans. People are still working to repair damage caused by Katrina.

Wind, rain, and floods from Hurricane Katrina in 2005 moved entire houses.

In October 2012, a storm formed in the ocean near Africa. It got bigger and stronger as it crossed the Atlantic Ocean and hit Cuba. Then it hit all the states along the eastern coast of the United States. It was called Super Storm Sandy. Storm surges flooded streets and subways. Some schools were closed for over a week while workers cleaned up flood damage.

 Was Super Storm Sandy a hurricane?

Homes in New York were flooded by Super Storm Sandy in 2012.

 Yes. It grew to a category 3 hurricane, but was a 1 when it hit the U.S. coast. It was called a super storm because it struck a large area.

A scientist at the National Hurricane Center studies the weather.

Q What makes hurricanes grow stronger?

Predicting Hurricanes

Meteorologists study storms and **predict** hurricanes. Weather **satellites** send photos of storms from space. Radar shows wind speed and rain. Meteorologists look at these reports. They study reports from older storms. This helps the National Hurricane Center predict storms. If a hurricane is likely, they send out warnings.

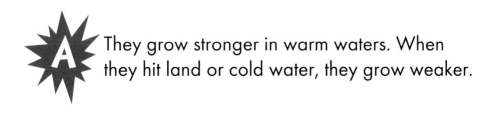

They grow stronger in warm waters. When they hit land or cold water, they grow weaker.

Hurricane hunters are special Air Force pilots. They fly into the eye of a hurricane. They measure wind speeds. They report the air temperature. Sometimes the pilots drop **buoys** into the water. The buoys measure the waves and wind. The reports go to the National Weather Service. These reports help meteorologists guess what the storm will do.

 When do hurricanes usually hit?

Pilots fly this WP-3D Orion plane into hurricanes to gather weather information.

 In the Atlantic Ocean, these storms usually hit from June 1 to November 30.

People in North Carolina put boards on their windows before a hurricane hits.

 Q Do hurricanes ever hit Canada?

Staying Safe

People on the seacoast should prepare for hurricanes. Make a plan. Find a way to connect with family. Maybe you have an aunt or uncle in another city. If so, everyone should have that person's number. That way, you can all check in and know where to meet.

 Very few hurricanes strike Canada. The ocean near Canada is cold. Hurricanes die out over cold water.

It is smart to listen to weather reports. A *hurricane watch* means a storm may come. A *hurricane warning* means a storm will come soon. You may need to leave the area. Check in with family in other towns. Lock the house. You will be safer away from the coast. Remember, hurricanes fizzle out over land.

Cars fill a Florida highway as people try to get away from the coast.

Glossary

buoy A floating marker in the ocean; hurricane buoys have tools to help measure wind and waves.

category A way to divide something into different groups; hurricanes are described by how strong they are.

cyclone Another name for a hurricane.

debris Broken pieces of buildings and landscape that have been destroyed.

eye wall The area outside of the eye of the hurricane.

meteorologist A scientist who studies the weather.

predict To tell in advance.

satellite An object that circles the earth in outer space collecting and sending data.

storm surge A huge wall of water along a coast caused by high winds.

Read More

Carson, Mary Kay. *Inside Hurricanes*. New York: Sterling, 2010.

Gregory, Josh. *The Superstorm Hurricane Sandy*. New York: Children's Press, 2013.

Person, Stephen. *Saving Animals from Hurricanes*. New York: Bearport, 2012.

Websites

Chris Kridler's Sky Diary | Hurricanes
skydiary.com/kids/hurricanes.html

Tropical Twisters | Hurricanes How They Work and What They Do
kids.earth.nasa.gov/archive/hurricane/

Weather WizKids | Hurricanes
www.weatherwizkids.com/weather-hurricane.htm

Index

About the Author

Elizabeth Raum has worked as a teacher, librarian, and writer. She says, "Storms are exciting." She has lived through blizzards and floods. She's seen a tornado in the distance. She watched earthquakes, hurricanes, and wildfires on the Weather Channel. It's safer! Visit her website at www.elizabethraum.net.